A SHORT FUNDAMENTAL GUIDE ON
HOW TO GET OUT OF YOUR HEAD,
OVERCOME YOUR FEARS AND
START A BUSINESS.

SHUT UP
AND START
THE D~~AMN~~
BUSINESS

By
NICCI CANADA

ReeseMcGhee Publishing

Shut Up and Start the Damn Business

A Short Fundamental Guide on How to Get Out of Your Head, Overcome Your Fears and Make Your Dreams A Reality.

ISBN 979-8-9870314-0-7

To my tribe.
Your love and support have been felt
throughout every part of my journey.

CONTENTS

CONTENTS

INTRODUCTION

If you need a 400-plus page book to be motivated, then this is definitely not for you. I contemplated writing this book because I initially felt I had to present a long book for others to be attracted to. The boringness of it all. Maybe I'll have more to say the next go around but this one is a mental jumpstart to going out there and starting a business. I didn't have mentors when I first started. What I did have was a plate of mistakes and I'm still making them, but I'm not a quitter. Starting a business can be scary if you don't know where to start. We have so many questions, unsure of who to talk to and who we can trust with our ideas. Trust me, I've been there.

So now you've decided to go for it, huh? You've recognized that there is more to you? You finally understood that you were placed in this realm to share your gifts, talents and abilities with the world and those around you? Or maybe you have a business, but the title of this book grabbed your attention? Maybe you're peeking in because you're interested in the thought of becoming an entrepreneur? Whatever the reason, the Team Greatness Squad welcomes you! There are people across the globe who support one another on this type of journey, so you are not alone. I want to see you living a fulfilled life, doing what you love and what you were placed on this earth to do. Why? Because I love you and your success is my success. Stop sitting on the sidelines envying others with regret. Tell "Fear" to kiss your ass, grab "I Can" by the hand and conquer the world together.

There are many levels to entrepreneurship. I want to give you the fundamentals to help you achieve success on this entrepreneur journey. There will be a lot of tweaking as you pursue your dreams, but the fact that you are reading this tells me that you are ready. It's your time!! Now close your eyes, take a deep breath and say, "I am worthy and ready to walk in greatness." Aaaahhhhh! That felt so good. It takes courage and I believe in you!

With Love,

Nicci Canada

WHO'S NICCI CANADA?

So who is Nicci Canada? A proud native of Charleston, West Virginia, who made my way to Charlotte, NC, where I've lived for the last 21 years. I'm a wife, mother, grandmother, entrepreneur, consultant and now author. I say that with a deep sigh. I wear many hats and honestly, I don't know how I do it all – but I was built for it. I'm not quite sure where to begin so I'll start from the beginning, or close to it. As early as thirteen years old I've had a love for people. I've always been intrigued by people's life stories and the journeys they've embarked upon to get to their successes. As a grown woman, nothing brings me more joy than seeing people live out their purpose.

In my early 20's I made a decision that would affect my life for some years to come. I was introduced to an opportunity to sell weed. It's laughable now because we're on the brink of having marijuana legalized in all states in America. One Saturday night, while out with a few college friends, I met a man named Paul in a night club back in Charleston. He gave me his number and told me he had a business opportunity for me. I was certain he was in the business of selling drugs, but I didn't care. It was something about the "opportunity" that excited me. In hindsight, it was the entrepreneur aspect of it that intrigued me.

Purchasing overhead, networking with clients, making the sale and experiencing happy, repeat customers. I was an entrepreneur back then; I just didn't know it because what was inside of me was not yet nurtured. My parents were both hard workers, going from lower class on government assistance to middle class. They taught me the value of money, the importance of good credit, how to save and to work hard for what you wanted, but there was still something I was searching for.

A week later, Paul came to my apartment. He was tall and very well-spoken with a thick, Jamaican accent and very confident in his presentation. He entered my little dwelling like Eddie Murphy playing the Prince of Zamunda in the movie "Coming to America." With an upright posture he sat in my living room chair next to the window showing off his gold pinky ring. He told me he was in the business of marijuana and that I could make some really good money selling it. When he left my apartment, I called a friend and told her what had happened. She asked me if I thought it, was a good idea. My response; Why not? Paul started teaching me the business, how to maintain my product and who to target. After a while, I didn't have to approach anyone; they all came to me. I could barely afford noodles in college; I didn't have a car or a job, so the money came in handy. Business was steady, but I didn't go overboard because I didn't want the attention. Unfortunately, attention came knocking anyway.

Two and a half years later, while visiting my sister, there was a knock at the door. Three men and a woman, all wearing FBI jackets, were standing outside with guns drawn, yelling for me to open the door. I swear it was like a movie, but I was staring in this one. I found myself behind bars, scared and knowing damn well I wasn't built for jail. All I could think about that night was my two-month-old son at home with my sister. As naïve as it sounds, I didn't think in a million years that I'd find myself in that situation; being interrogated by the FBI for hours and asking me the same questions over and over again, like they didn't hear me the first time. And then trying to pin things on me that I had absolutely nothing to do with was exhausting. Less than a day in jail was definitely enough for me. On sentencing day, 13 months later, my lawyer informed me that my charges were negotiated and I'd serve one year in jail. I was sick to say the least, but it beat the five years I was initially looking to serve. There were a few other women who got involved with Paul and unfortunately, they weren't so lucky. They went away for five plus years, leaving children behind, and I've often wondered how those women turned out. A year wasn't that long, but the thought of me leaving my son devastated me. His father was already in prison for drug charges and I was ashamed for having put my parents through all of this.

After the meeting with my lawyer, we went back into the courtroom for sentencing. The judge proceeded to tell me about the one year sentence and then his words were followed by complete silence. He started looking over some papers and changed his mind. He gave me 6 months house arrest and 5 years' probation. My dad was behind me thanking Jesus while I was standing there trying to figure out what just happened. It was a sigh of relief to say the least. I did, however, end up with some felonies on my record and this ruined my life, or so I thought. Let's just say it made things very difficult for several years. I can't stress enough counting the cost of every decision that you make because it can yield consequences that are beyond your control.

Even though I was on house arrest, I went back to college, enrolled my son into daycare and got a part-time job at the hospital working as a "runner" in the mailroom. My mother knew a professor on campus who put in a good word for me. To this day, I'm always tickled at the memories I had working there with that ankle monitor on. All the stares I'd get, but no one said a word. I worked there for two years until I completed school. It was tough going to school and working as a single mother, but the help of family got me through. I finished out at the Huntington Junior College of Business as a Medical Technician with a Certificate in Business.

Once I graduated from college things started to get a little interesting. I moved to Maryland and got a job working as a Medical Technician in a pediatric office. I would often lie on my applications when I applied for a job. I got so tired of answering that question; "Have you ever been convicted of a felony?" Whenever I answered yes to that question, I was immediately denied so I figured I'd roll the dice and lie on this one. I worked there for a year and moved back to West Virginia because my sister needed me. I then realized that the medical field was not for me. I was tired of dealing with whiny parents who were actually worse than the sick children they were bringing in. Returning home, I ended up working at the state tax department. I know, right? A good friend of the family got me that job. My felonies were a hush; I went to work every day and minded my own business. From there, I got married and moved to North Carolina. The beginning of the marriage was a struggle. I was still on probation and moving to another state required me to find a job within six months or I would have to return back to West Virginia.

Me being unable to land employment caused a lot of stress, frustration and depression. My felonies didn't define me but I was definitely suffering from my choices. I was pregnant again with my second son and sometimes we only had ten dollars left to our name after the bills were paid.....Literally. Everywhere I went they required background checks and the better-paying jobs like the bank and postal service demanded fingerprints; I was quickly denied for those. Time was winding down so I decided to write the judge who sentenced me back home. I wrote a nine-page letter explaining my situation and that I did in fact make some wrong choices, but I didn't want that to define me. I had asked if he would grant me an early release from probation so I could move forward with my new life here in North Carolina with my family. A few weeks later I received a letter granting me an early release from probation. Yes!!

Still determined, I continued to look for work. I eventually landed a job as a waitress. It was hard work, but it helped to bring in extra money for the bills. That job ended because they didn't want to work with my schedule and the need to be home with the kids when my husband was at work. I eventually applied for a position at a grocery store in the produce section. After a few days I went back to the store to speak with the hiring manager. When I asked about the position, he awkwardly began to stutter. I knew what he wanted to say, so I finished his sentence for him. He apologized and told me he couldn't hire me because of my background. For real?!!!! Like really?!!! I applied for a position in the produce section handling fruits and veggies. It wasn't that serious! I went back to my car and cried in that parking lot for over an hour. I was screaming, yelling and cursing everything, including God. I was tired of being told no over and over again; tired of being honest but getting nowhere and tired of being judged by my past mistakes—then one day I decided to start my own business.

Dreaming is cool, but you
have to wake up and make
your dreams a reality.

- Nicci Canada

GET OUT OF YOUR HEAD

I always considered it a serious crime when one chooses not to follow their dreams or share their gifts and talents with those around them. When you have a gift, that gift does not belong to you. It belongs to me and others whom you were meant to serve with it. So how dare you hoard what's inside of you. How dare you take it upon yourself to decide you will not operate in your talents, gifts and abilities. Think of all the people who have impacted you in your life and imagine if they would have hoarded their gifts, talents or abilities. Imagine that. When someone has a gift for someone but refuses to give it to them, I would consider that person to be very selfish because it doesn't belong to you; it belongs to me, to us, the world! And what does this have to do with starting a business? Everything. Your gifts, talents and abilities are all tied into what you're actually good at. These are your money makers!

Along this journey I've encountered hundreds of people who are always in their head. Whenever I meet a stranger, I'm quick to ask what they do and what their hobbies and dreams are. This excites me, listening to others' ideas and me envisioning them manifest. Many aren't sure of what they're good at or they have several ideas, but that's all they are—

ideas. Once I hear their ideas, I usually follow up with a simple question. What's stopping you? I'd hear repeatedly about how they wish or they aren't sure, or if they just had this. Whenever I'd hear this, all I heard were excuses. But then one day I thought to myself, maybe they weren't all excuses, but rather the lack of understanding and knowledge mixed with fear. Some really want to get out of their head but lack the resources, or don't know how to get unstuck, or maybe they need that extra push to get them on the right track. I've been on my entrepreneur journey for 17 years and one thing I've learned is that you have to get out of your head and just do it! Take one step at a time and do the damn thing.

Believe it or not we all possess a superhuman power: the power to create. We seem to ignore or forget this power even though we practice it every day. A lot of times to our detriment but none the less this superpower still exists. This is an area of your life that must be nurtured and mastered. When thought meets belief, activated with faith, you've got a force to be reckoned with. You'll be unstoppable with those ideas once they're manifested in this realm. Now, you may have heard this countless times, or it might be your first, but everything begins with a thought. It sounds so cliché because people say it all the time. But do you really believe it? If you do believe it, are you practicing this truth? Or are you an imposter? Everything that you see around you began with someone thinking it into existence. Good or bad, they are all thoughts. Not only were they thoughts, they nurtured the thoughts, so much so that you now enjoy or suffer from millions of "thoughts" we see around us every day. Now that's an amazing superpower.

So, what is it? What are your thoughts? What is it that fulfills and energizes you when you're doing what you love? For some, this is a hard question. I've heard countless times from people that they don't know what they're good at. But that's okay! The days of you sitting around in the shadows, watching everyone else is over. You've had ideas twirling around in that brain of yours for years and never acted upon or even spoke of them. But now we're going to get those ideas out of your head so you can start the damn business!

My first business was a cleaning business. I was always a neat freak and great at organizing things, so I decided to make money doing what I was good at. While preparing for my new adventure, I got a job working for a cleaning company making $15.00 an hour as an independent contractor. No necessary background checks were a positive, but it wasn't a lot of money considering I was responsible for my own cleaning supplies, and taxes. I took the job because I wanted to learn the business and see how my boss - at the time - ran hers. I did such a great job that a lot of her clients were requesting me instead of her other workers. This is when things started to change. I collected checks from clients after every service and was required to submit those checks to my boss at the end of the week. I remember waking up that Friday morning with this weird feeling that I was going to get fired. I went into the office, handed her the checks and she looked me dead in my face and told me that she was intimidated by me (yes, those were her exact words), and that she was letting me go. I remember saying to her that I was a good worker and I never once took any of her clients. She wished me luck, put her head down and started counting her money. JUST LIKE THAT!! She didn't say another word.

This was an extremely bad time in my life because me and my husband were struggling financially, and I needed to bring in extra money for the household. We had two young children at the time, and it was very stressful. I went back to my car (the den of tears), cried for about ten minutes, only to realize why I started working for this woman in the first place. I wanted to learn the cleaning business and my mission was accomplished! I had everything I needed! I paid attention to her marketing strategies, her decision to deal with contractors instead of employees, pricing, customer service, everything. And this was all done through observation and hands-on experience. The only thing I didn't take with me were her clients. I respected that because I wanted the same respect from those who would work for me. With the expertise I had received from working that job, I was confident in starting my own cleaning business.

WHAT IS YOUR WHY?

We all have different reasons for wanting to start our own business. Freedom, generational wealth, second income. What's yours? Freedom and generational wealth are my why. I also want to travel the world and experience life from a different perspective. My grandparents on both sides were entrepreneurs. My maternal grandparents were James and Esther McGhee. James dipped and dabbled in several things. He was a singer, brick mason, barber and owner of a small taxi service. I remember as a teenager, my grandfather would park his gray station wagon next to an outdoor payphone near the railroad tracks and wait for the phone to ring. My grandmother, Esther, owned a juke-joint called "The Stand". For those who aren't familiar with the term, a juke joint was often a small run-down building on the out skirts of town. As a young girl, I remember "The Stand" being frequented by locals stopping in to socialize, drink and smoke while enjoying the sounds of an old dusty juke box playing music from country to rhythm and blues.

My grandparents on my father's side were Sam and Gladys Reese. I never met my grandfather, Sam, also a barber, who died a year before I was born but I always listened attentively when my grandmother spoke of him. Gladys was a very prominent woman in my life. She managed a café called VFW in downtown Charleston, WV and eventually left the café and retired as a cook for Job Corp. Gladys was "mean" in the kitchen and to experience her fried chicken, greens and homemade rolls was as close as you would get to meeting God. Alongside her talent for cooking, Gladys was a very business-oriented woman who kept her affairs in order until death. Both of my grandmothers were tough, hardworking women. Esther was rough around the edges, drank her liquor, played the guitar and was free-spirited. Gladys was more poised, a tad bit bougie and somewhat opposite of Esther, but their presentations were both beautiful in my eyes. I was very intrigued about what my grandparents did and the stories they told, but they all died broke except for Gladys. When she passed, she left me and my siblings $1,000 each. While that may not have been a lot to some, she left us with something, and I am by no means speaking down on my other grandparents. James and Esther didn't leave monetary possessions, but they damn sure left priceless knowledge and beautiful memories; something I will cherish for the rest of my life. Gladys was the last grandparent to transition, and my "why" became more apparent after her death. I wanted to leave something to my offspring. I wanted to make sure that my grandchildren were left with enough money to start their own businesses and be able to benefit financially from something I created in this lifetime. I now wake up every morning driven by my why. What's yours?

TALENT & SKILL

Oftentimes, our direction, dreams and purpose are tied in with the talents and skills we possess. Do you know what talents and skills you have? People get confused by these terms and often believe they mean the same thing. Talents and skills are actually different. A talent is a special ability to do something possessed by a person naturally. It is something that you do best without putting extra effort into it, and we see these special talents manifest quite early in one's life. Children, when given permission to express themselves and be free, will often engage in activities they like the most or excel in. Their talent is then nurtured and developed properly, normally through coaching. People's talents can sometimes go "undiscovered" because they weren't given permission to express themselves, or there was a lack of support or guidance. This understanding has helped me to understand those who don't know what their talents are. A skill, on the other hand, is not "God given" but something you acquire through learned behavior, hard work, practice, time and effort. I've known several who have the same ability; for example, singing. One person was born with this ability as it came very natural to them. The other didn't have this born-given talent, but they became good at it through hard work and practice. Talent and skill are cousins and when the two merge, magic happens!

Another comparison of talent and skill.

Basis For Comparison	Talent	Skill
Meaning	Talent in an inherent ability of a person to do something.	Skill is the expertise to do a particular task efficiently.
What is it?	It's something God gifted.	It is something you develop.
Possessed by	Few people only	Anyone can possess it through learning.
Requires	Recognition	Development
Guidance	Coaching	Training
		Source: Starttech

Usually, your talents will look different from someone else you know. We often associate scientists as "talented geniuses" while looking down on someone who waits tables. Most likely, if you place a scientist in a hospitality position, they may find a job like this extremely challenging. Why? Because scientists don't normally carry the hospitality "gene". Those who carry the hospitality gene could go on to become an event planner, start a concierge service, a travel company or a catering company. A scientist could start a manufacturing company dealing with chemicals, biomedical devices, or as an atmospheric scientist doing research on climate change. Understand the difference? Now let's find out what you're good at. Below is a small list of talents and skills. I encourage you to do some more research on the many talents, along with skills, that are out there.

Examples of Talents and Skills

· Story Telling	· Writing
· Building Things	· Networking
· Multi-Lingual	· Dancing
· Singing	· Time Management
· Planning	· Marketing
· Teaching	· Problem Solving
· Mathematical Thinking	· Creating Thinking
· Graphic Design/Drawing	· Time Management
· Communication	· Adaptability
· Public Speaking	· Computers
· Resourcefulness	· Organization
· Cooking	· Caring for others

Now that you have a better understanding of talent and skill, write yours down below or use a notebook.

Talents: What are you naturally good at?

1._____

2._____

3._____

4._____

Skills: What non-talent have you perfected or are perfecting?

1._____

2._____

3._____

4._____

Do you have a story to tell? Write a book and sell it on a media platform like I did. Are you good at editing and capturing video content? Promote your services to companies looking for your talent. Do you have a product that would be great for consumers? Test the market and sell it! Do you have an idea for an app that could solve problems? Solve it! Do you have a mobile service that would be great in your area? Go for it! Do you have a passion for youth? Start a camp or an academy. Can you repair computers? Service companies for a monthly fee. Are you gifted in coding and want to teach kids? Do the damn thang! Whatever it is, get the word out and get paid!

STRENGTHS & WEAKNESSES

N ow before we get to the juicy part about those wonderful business ideas floating around in your head, let's discuss strengths and weaknesses. This section might not be for you if you're without any weakness. In fact, you should just skip this section completely. If you're reading this basking in perfection, your words and presentation are magical and fairy dust falls to the ground every time you walk, this section will not be very helpful.

Regarding strengths, I'm a fast learner, detail-oriented, very determined and very creative. I love to design and develop concepts. Not having mentors, when I started with very little resources, challenged me to learn quickly, pay attention and study things I didn't know. One of my weaknesses was perfection; and boy did I have it bad. It took me a while before I addressed this particular one and it made things a lot harder for me. I was always overthinking and feeling like my work wasn't good enough. I'm good at designing websites, flyers, etc. and it was nothing for me to spend weeks on something that should have only taken a day or two. I had to learn that nothing is perfect and never will be. I'm now learning to go with it and perfect as I go.

Networking was another weakness of mine. I found it awkward walking up to strangers at an event discussing my business. It felt like small talk and made me uncomfortable. I've always been into deep conversations, discussing the sun, moon, stars, fifth dimension and weird things that may or may not exist. I never considered myself to be shy, so I couldn't understand this fear. I avoided networking events like the plague and wanted nothing to do with it, but soon discovered that networking was imperative!! Someone once told me, "You have to network to get work" and this is so true. Sometimes your solution lies within the person you're talking to, or they may know someone who can connect the dots in helping to expand your company. I admired my strengths, but my weaknesses were causing me to be stagnant in my business.

Weaknesses are something we should improve on. Writing was definitely not a strength of mine. I did, however, start to face my fears, and here we are; my first book! Had I not gotten over that fear, you wouldn't be reading this right now. It's not nearly as perfect as I would like it to be, but I did it and will become better as I continue to write and perfect the skill. Weaknesses can and do turn into strengths when we decide that we want to embrace our better self.

Knowing your strengths and weaknesses matter! Why?

- It helps to develop more self-awareness.
- It helps to develop more confidence.
- You can better communicate with others around you.
- It helps better define your direction in life.
- It helps you better navigate your own business.

Examples of Strengths:

- Enthusiasm
- Communication
- Open Minded
- Patience
- Independent
- Determination

Examples of weakness:

- Being a perfectionist
- Procrastination
- Unorganized
- Impatient
- People pleaser
- Unhealthy habits

What are your Strengths & Weaknesses? Write them down below

Strengths:

1. _____

2. _____

3. _____

4. _____

5. _____

Weaknesses:

1. _____

2. _____

3. _____

4. _____

5. _____

Notes: _____

_____

_____

_____

_____

_____

Field Assignment

Your next assignment is to ask friends, family and associates what they consider to be your talents, strengths, weaknesses. You may already know what these are, but it would still be beneficial to ask others. Let's see if these match with what you have written down. Be sure to ask those you trust to tell you the honest truth.

THE POWER OF DECISION

$$\bullet \cdot \circledast \cdot \bullet$$

Now here's the fun part! I want you to take your "magic wand" and write down every idea you have for a possible business. There is nothing that sounds too farfetched, silly or stupid. Write it all down. I don't care if you want a mobile service that gives people baths and shaves every last piece of hair off their body. Write it down. This exercise is not something that needs to be done immediately. It may take a few days or even weeks. Please, take the time needed to fill out your list. Oftentimes we overlook the greatness within because it's second nature to us. We do it so naturally that we don't even recognize what we have. You might already be operating in your talents but never considered the possibility of getting paid for it. Your gifts are your money-makers. Secure the bag.

Juicy Bit:

Always keep paper and pen handy. Sometimes great ideas seem to fall out of the sky. You could be meditating, exercising, washing dishes, feeding the dog, taking a bath or mowing the lawn. For those who don't use a pen and paper, take notes on your phone or tablet. Whatever is best for you. Just write it down!

Okay.... Let's Go! It's time to write. If you need to pause reading this book and come back in a few days, it's perfectly fine to do so and I encourage it if needed. If you were able to get those ideas out of your head, feel free to use the space I have created for you to write down your ideas.

Business Ideas:

1. _____

2. _____

3. _____

4. _____

5. _____

Notes: _____

_____

_____

_____

_____

_____

First, I'm proud that you wrote it all down. Many keep their ideas a secret for years; so much of a secret that you won't discuss it with yourself. Now take a good look at your list. Look at all the ideas that came from such an amazing person. You did that! "But Nicci, how do I choose from this list?!" I'm glad you asked. What ideas on your list compliment your talents, skills, strengths, passion and experience? You don't need to be an expert, but your talent and skill will increase your chances of success with the business that you choose.

Now that you have your business ideas jotted down with a better understanding of what your talents, gifts, strengths and weaknesses are, it's time to decide. Nothing will slow you down more than to be all over the place having your hands in everything and busy doing nothing. You need to decide on an idea and focus. Having a bunch of businesses bringing in very little seems like overkill when you can put that same amount of energy into one business and make magic happen. Everything will come in due time, but for now decide what you want to pursue, why you want to pursue it and how. These are all important and writing these things down will help you stay focused. Speaking of focus, that was also a major weakness of mine that I'm learning to master. As a creator, my mind is always wandering. I sit and think about ideas all day and if I'm not careful, I'm scattered all over the place. For one, I still write out my ideas in my little black book; second, I understand that they are ideas and timing is important; and third, if it's meant to manifest, it will in due time. I'm still going to remain focused on what I currently have and create success from it.

Throughout your entrepreneurial journey you'll learn that some things are good ideas and "God' ideas. Good ideas sound awesome at first. Your adrenaline is at an all-time high, it "sounds good" but it just doesn't sit well. You're not really passionate about it and end up showing very little interest in it. I took over a business selling eyelashes. It sounded like a good idea at first. I invested a little over $1,500 but quickly realized that I had very little interest and let it go. I even had a hard time telling strangers about what I had to offer. So, if I was reluctant to tell potential customers about a product of mine, then I was definitely doing something wrong. Needless to say, I felt stupid, and as a friend of mine so eloquently put it, it was an attempted failure. I was side-eyed when he said it, but he was telling the truth and it taught me a valuable lesson, or so I thought. I love beauty products as a consumer, but I took no passion in selling them.

Unfortunately, I still hadn't learned my lesson because I came up with this genius idea to sell lip balm. I received my first bulk order from a franchise and was on top of the world. It started off good. I then added candles and soaps and quickly realized that I didn't enjoy that either. I'm a lip balm junkie and moisturized lips are a must for me—but to sell it? I like to burn candles, but I damn sure didn't enjoy selling them. I'm in the kitchen trying to learn how to make candles and soon realized that candle making was a science with love sprinkled on top. Certain waxes don't work with certain fragrances; you must have the correct wick(s) depending on the size of the candle; you have to pour your fragrances at a certain temperature, and none of these truths were the same for every candle type. It was the worst experience ever and I'm reminded of it whenever I open my kitchen cabinet and see those supplies collecting dust. I then decided to pay someone else to make the candles, but I still wasn't happy. I found no fulfillment in that business whatsoever. It was like pulling teeth. I'd sit in my office looking at all these products only to sell most of them for cheap to recoup some of the money I had invested into the business. To me, these were all good ideas that didn't work for me. The "God" idea would eventually present itself.

Five years from now will come soon; success or procrastination will meet you there.

- Nicci Canada

OPPORTUNITIES & OBSTACLES

Time stops for no one. Imagine if you had been consistent in one area for the last 3-5 years. Where would you be? The big picture or end result should be your motivation, but there will be obstacles that you must conquer and nothing happens overnight. Being an entrepreneur does come with pros and cons, but this should not deter you from going out there and making it happen.

Pros

- **You Work for Yourself** – You are your own boss; you call the shots and make the final decisions related to running your business. And no more working for people you don't like.

- **Flexible Schedule** – This is one of my favorite pros of becoming an entrepreneur. You get to choose the days and hours you work. This allows you to give more attention to your personal life and other commitments.

- **You're More Passionate About What You Do** – You can turn your passion, talents and strengths into a business while making money doing what you love. I'd rather this option than passing my ideas to an employer where they get all the credit and give me a bonus if I'm lucky.

- **Your Revenue Bag Has Unlimited Potential** – The amount of money you earn is completely up to you, since you pay yourself. Doesn't that sound good? It sounds wonderful to me.

- **Freedom to Travel** – You're free to leave the country for a month, if you like, as long as your business and finances are in order. And depending on your type of work, you can work remotely while traveling.

Cons

- **You Must Be Disciplined** - For your business to grow, you must be in control of your time and finances. Don't misuse the funds from your business for personal needs.

- **Your Progress Can Be Slow** – I've said it before; nothing comes overnight. This is a slow steady grind and money may not come rushing in like the person you follow on Instagram who became a millionaire in six days.

- **You're Responsible for All Losses** – Every loss you take will belong to you and you need to have back up money to cover these losses.

- **You work longer hours** – While you definitely can choose your own hours, you'll be working longer hours. Your business will require a lot of attention for it to grow.

- **You have to perform all duties/functions within your business** – Don't be fooled. Unless you can afford to outsource your work to others, you'll be the salesperson, marketer, designer, accountant, administrator and representative. #TeamSeveralHats

But this can't stop you! There's a reason why you're reading this book and have gotten this far. Start the Damn Business!

ARE YOU READY?

So now you have your business idea and you're ready to go out there and do the damn thing! I'm so proud of you! I'm proud that you took the first step to seeing your dreams come to life in this realm. Fear is something that we've all dealt with and will experience on occasion. It's absolutely normal. To be a successful business owner, despite your reservations and certain fears, you must be courageous enough to jump off the mountain with a "greatness cape" expecting something great to happen. Let's face it, you have to jump in order to fly. Fear is normal and can be very healthy. You may be ready to go all in or there may be something that's stopping you from starting in the first place. What are you scared of? Scared of other people's opinions? Scared to disappoint your family and friends? Not good at selling? Scared you won't have enough money to live on? Scared no one will buy your product? I was taught two types of fear; fear that can save you from physical harm, such as a venomous snake that pops out of a bush and you haul ass up the street in 2.5 seconds. This is a healthy fear that saves you from harm or possible death. Then there's fear that paralyzes you from setting goals, walking out your purpose or following your dreams. Yes, we all have fears, but I need you to push beyond your fears!

In overcoming your fears and starting your business, there are a few things I need you to understand:

- Keep your mouth shut about your ideas (outside of people you trust).

- Get used to the word no. "No's" will eventually lead to "yes."

- This is your dream; it doesn't belong to anyone else but you.

- Celebrate the small goals.

- There will be days when you will absolutely want to quit. Keep going.

- Your family members may not support you or even believe in you. Keep going.

- Some that have the means to help you may not do so. Keep going!

- There is no such thing as an overnight success.

- You will absolutely make mistakes, but the only way you'll get better is to keep going.

- There is nothing wrong with being inspired, but don't compare yourself to others.

- Kill the chatter of doubt that will constantly try to creep in and deter you from accomplishing your dream.

- Stay focused! Oftentimes when things aren't going right in your business, you'll get sidetracked with another "bright idea" that will take you off the path.

- Enjoy the journey! Good, bad and ugly.

As I stated above, keep your lips closed about everything you do as it pertains to your business unless you're sharing with a team of trusted advisors. Don't be afraid to require those whom you discuss business with to sign a non-disclosure agreement. It's basically a legally binding contract establishing confidentiality where the party is bound to keep their mouth closed concerning your business.

Show people better than you can tell them. Let them watch while you work and put your money where your mouth is. Some are looking to steal your ideas because they haven't tapped into their creativity; they'll not only take your ideas but will sabotage what you have because they don't believe in what you're doing. Be very mindful of those who project their fears onto you; you'll find yourself delaying the process or not starting. This happens when you're still combating fears and insecurities within yourself.

Out of everyone in the world, we all want support from family and friends. That wasn't always the case for me. Some of my family members and close friends never brought a product or admission ticket from me. I used to take it personally, but I soon realized that regardless of who was supporting me I had to want it bad enough for myself. If you crumble because no one is supporting you, in your circle of friends and family, then you don't want it bad enough. Simply put, you're not built for this. Go back to the "security" of a nine to five because not everyone will support you.

Getting used to the word no is definitely something that I cannot express enough; therefore, I need you to get used to the different variations of the word "No."

Let's practice, shall we?

- No
- Nah
- Nope
- I'm good

- No, thank you
- I'm not interested
- The call abruptly ends (because they hung up on your ass…lol)
- I'll pass.
- Maybe some other time.
- Call me next week (they won't answer the phone).
- I'll think about it (…and they still won't answer the phone).

THIS IS GOING TO HAPPEN!!

How silly of me to think that everyone would love what I had to offer. How could anyone say no to me? Who do they think they are? I'm a nice person, I'm honest, my services are great, blah, blah, blah. Get over it. Unless you have something innovative, and that has its challenges as well, you're competing with hundreds—if not thousands—of other people in the same field. Depending on where you're located, competition can be very minimal and that's a good thing. Remember, this is business, and your soft, mushy feelings have no place in the business world. So what if someone sells apples down the street? Make your apples juicy and irresistible. Create the illusion that your apples are floating on air. Most buy the experience and not the product anyway. The best advice I can give you in this area is to be consistent, work on your business every day, don't take no for an answer and believe in your product or services.

Now let's touch on the word passion for a quick second. It's loosely thrown around, but simply put, passion is your gas/drive. It takes gas to drive a car so without gas the car goes nowhere. This also applies to your business ideas. If there is no passion for what it is that you're thinking about doing, your business will die. It may start off good but will eventually wither because the passion was never there. Passion is what will get you through tough times, times when your business doesn't seem to be doing well. Passion allows you to keep going because you believe in what you're doing, and you refuse to quit. Everyone will not see the vision or have the passion for what you do. Accepting this truth will save you a lot of heartache. There will, however, be people who will come into your life and help you along your journey. I honestly should have documented the no's along mine. I've encountered some who had the resources to help me but chose not to. I didn't want to accept this truth, but there were some that were just plain jealous around their assumption that I was doing better than them.

I was out here busting my ass trying to figure it out like the next person; asking our church to help with groceries, Christmas toys and even visiting local food pantries. My parents would help out whenever possible and even through the struggle I was still determined to go out here and create something. Now let's be clear, everyone wasn't jealous of me. Sometimes the doors would intentionally slam in my face because my product and services needed tweaking or weren't appealing. There are many reasons the train is not moving the way you want it to. In hindsight, I'm thankful for the doors that were closed in my face. It built resilience, determination and patience. It made me stronger; it fueled my ambition and has created someone who's so determined to accomplish my dreams and goals. I have sacrificed so much to get where I'm headed, and I wouldn't change any of it.

Another disappointment was silly me thinking that I would be an overnight success. Here's the raw truth: some of the things that are now manifesting in my business were penned fifteen years ago. Fifteen Years!!!! Stop allowing social media to deceive you. All you see is overnight success without countless nights of tears and frustration. For some it may take five to ten years or more, but the message is to be consistent with what you believe in. So, what is Success? According to Oxford English dictionary, success is the accomplishment of an aim or purpose. Goals that you set within your business lead to your success and it's up to you to determine your level of success; as this looks different for many.

Let's say Lamar always had a dream to open a business lounge with a café. He wants to keep it local at one location from Monday-Friday; 8am-8pm. This may be his level of success and if he accomplishes this, he is successful! Kimyata wants to sell handmade jewelry to wealthy clients. She didn't want a store; she wanted to remain mobile and keep it exclusive. If she accomplished this goal, she was successful. Steven loves the real estate industry and wants to own and rent out ten residential properties and five event spaces in his local and surrounding area. Once again, if he accomplishes this, he is successful with his goals.

Don't compare your dreams and goals to others. Everyone will not be a Robert Smith, Sheila Johnson, Jeff Bezos, Oprah Winfrey, Rihanna or David Steward. Now don't get me wrong, these people are great inspirations and their experiences are something you can most certainly glean from. This doesn't mean that you can't be prosperous and successful. It's trillions of dollars out here in circulation. Decide what your cut will be through services or products offered to the masses with dedication, consistency and a plan. Planet Neptune is the limit, baby!

MONEY GOALS & WOES

Now we must address your startup capital. Startup capital is money used to pay for expenses needed to start your business. These funds help with initial costs, such as registration, licensing, supplies, equipment, marketing, space, or any other expense needed to operate the business. But how much? Your startup costs are determined by what's needed to get going. Some businesses require very little overhead while others need a lot to get going. A freelance job as a virtual assistant would require less overhead than someone who wants to open a café. Research your line of work and educate yourself on what's needed to start the business so you have a clear number in your head to move forward. Startup costs can deter people from getting started because they aren't sure of where the money will come from.

For some:

- You're wearing your startup capital because you won't stop shopping.

- You're driving in your startup capital because you need to impress others around you, so you purchase the car you wanted but didn't need.

- You're vacationing with your startup capital because you always have to get away.

- You eat out every weekend and spend frivolously on unnecessary bs.

- You pay child support and extra day care fees with your startup capital because of ignorant, heat-of-the moment decisions. Our babies are blessings but make better choices.

- You're married to or dating your startup capital. Be careful who you link up with; that person could stand in your way of becoming successful. Choose wisely; outside of love, marriage is also a business transaction.

Is there a sacrifice to be made? Yes!!! A lot of us weren't born into money or have readily available resources to flourish. You have to decide what you want in life because, honestly speaking, outside of that warm, fuzzy little circle you call friends and family, no one cares about you. People have good intentions, but at the end of the day they have their own problems and dreams to contend with.

After I was fired from that cleaning job, I planned things out a few more months and studied other cleaning companies while working at a laundromat making five dollars an hour under the table. It was the best I could do because we couldn't afford day care. I was, however, allowed to bring my sons to work and it was within walking distance from our apartment. I saved $200, created some flyers, brought some cleaning supplies and cleaned houses in the morning before my husband went to work in the afternoon. I made $23k my first year with a bucket, vacuum and supplies. It's not going to be perfect, but start the damn business. Although my planning was choppy at the beginning, I eventually learned as I went. Again, it's important that you write down what your overhead cost will be to start the business. This cost is determined by what's needed to run your business and there will be resources at the end of this book to help you.

Being worried about money is quite common because we have this big dream but are unsure of how it can be accomplished without it. Several ways to obtain funds for your business are:

- Personal Savings (Start putting away money to help with your start-up costs)

- Small Business Loans/Grants (Do your research)

- Barter Services - Use your talents and skills in exchange for something you need accomplished in your business.

- Raising funds (friends, family, yard sales, bake sales, selling things on retail platforms)

Juicy Bit: Give yourself six months to a year to plan your business out properly as well as save up for things needed.

As your business begins to grow you must resist the urge to spend. I made that mistake when I opened my cleaning business. I was making $50-$150 an hour cleaning houses. The money was good, but I never invested back into my company. The money I was making could have been better spent on marketing and staffing to expand the company. I didn't know any better at the time, and I wish I'd had a mentor to sit me down and tell me I was about to crash and burn. I mismanaged those funds and ended up being an employee of my own business, working by myself with no more contractors on staff. The passion was no longer there as my focus was more on following my dreams as a singer in the entertainment industry. What was once a goal of having a successful cleaning company with staff and company cars became a distant memory. It was then, after thirteen years, that I decided to let the business go.

The music industry then became my full-time passion. Shows were picking up and I had a chance to travel some within the U.S doing what I loved to do. When the opportunity presented itself for me to sing with the Charleston Pops Orchestra and the Tulsa Pops Orchestra. It was something beyond what I had ever expected. I recorded an album that gained very little traction here in the U.S. but in the United Kingdom, mom and pop shops purchased my albums from me wholesale and sold them to their customers. That was another stream of income that definitely came in handy. I never thought I'd see an album that I recorded in another country being sold. It was such a great accomplishment! From there I went on to start my own production company, Dapper Street Productions. As a professional jazz singer who booked and marketed my own services for many years, I understood the music business and how things flowed. It was rather easy to start an entertainment company because of that knowledge. I understood the ins and outs from a business standpoint, so as a musician it was an easy transition because I was already doing it. This is why it's good to embrace your skill sets, passions, gifts, talents and abilities, because somewhere within that formula lies the God Idea! I had finally tapped into my "God Idea"! I went from asking others to be on their stage to producing my own shows and creating a stage for other artists.

I quickly told myself that I wouldn't make the same mistake that I made the first time around. Almost every penny I made went back into my company or was put away and I was better prepared to deal with the costs needed to grow the business. The economic shut down due to the Covid-19 pandemic was really a test of all the things I had learned. With a cushion of $25k in the bank to invest more into my company, it put me at a better advantage. When Dapper Street temporarily shut down, I was faced with the option of riding out the wave with the capital I had saved or getting a job to help take care of necessities at home. I got a job working for Amazon and went from having the freedom to come and go as I pleased, to working 40 plus hours a week. I had to write out my schedule of what was needed to get done on my days off and goals to accomplish in the evening when I got home from work.

Working 10-hour shifts and coming home to work on my own business was mentally exhausting to say the least.

On your days off, commit to working on your dream, even if it's for one hour in the morning or evening. Just be consistent. Is it easy? No! But when you have a dream, nothing should stop you. My consistency has allowed me to see my business grow even with setbacks. Don't worry about others or how fast they're moving. A lot of growth takes place behind the scenes. There will be a harvest, but first you must plant seeds.

LAW & ORDER

I'll assume that your organizational skills are on point and you never have issues, but if not, you'll bring problems to your door that could jeopardize your business. Again, I'll give you information at the end of this book to help you. With that said, your business shouldn't be scattered all over the place. There should be a designated place within your home/office where all your business documents, receipts, tax returns, etc. are stored. Make a habit of spending a few days a month filing paperwork and updating your accounting information. This way you're not scrambling around trying to prepare for tax season. It can be a very stressful time of the year if you're not organized. Make sure you have proper licenses, permits, credentials, tax id number and bank accounts set up in your company name and never use a personal bank account to handle your affairs. Overwhelming, right? It can be, but being organized will make your life so much better. When I first started, I documented everything in a little black book. All my spending, payroll, monies earned, everything. That was the only thing that worked for me at the time. I didn't know the power of an excel sheet nor did I know how to use one. There's honestly no excuse as to why someone can't run their business properly with all the apps and software we have now at affordable prices. Androids and iPhones have literally become virtual offices to make your business run smoother. Take advantage of it.

I don't get distracted
easily; I just have a lot to....
oh look, shiny things!

- Unknown

SHINY THINGS

Now you're finally putting in work; street hustling, networking, cold calls, door-to-door sales, target marketing ads and countless emails but can't seem to catch a break. I found myself getting distracted and venturing off trying other business opportunities when things weren't going well. Hindsight, this is how I ended up selling lip balm, candles and other shiny objects that were taking me away from what I needed to focus on. Earlier in my entrepreneur career I used to get involved in network marketing opportunities. These companies seemed promising and had me feeling like I'd be a millionaire in the next two years. I'd entertain these new ventures for a while but would quit because I wasn't making any money. Eventually I'd end up running back to my own business picking up where I left things. The instability and addiction to shiny things were becoming a detriment to my success. Discipline, focus and consistency are three major things one must have to achieve success.

If you're flat out lazy, enjoy going out all the time, spending countless hours on social media, partying, and tv binge-watching, you will never accomplish your goals or fulfill your dreams. Focus on your nine to five because you clearly don't want it bad enough. I cut out social media for several months to get myself together and accelerate my goals. Social media had me so distracted that I hardly got anything done. I should have already written five books with the time I wasted on social media throughout the years. A lot of things on my "to do" list could have been accomplished if it weren't for all the binge-watching I was doing on these popular movie apps. What are you willing to sacrifice to start your business? Being single with no children puts you at an advantage as an entrepreneur because you don't have that added responsibility. I do, however, see people responsible for their families outworking those who are single.

If you're serious, set aside a block of time to commit to your business every day, even if only for an hour. Don't feel a certain way because you cannot commit 100%. Let that mindset go unless you're going to quit your day job and go for it. Some are in a position to tell their bosses to eat dirt because they've saved enough money to quit or there's a second stream of income from a spouse or significant other. If that's not your situation, then go easy on yourself! Nothing is going to be perfect; you will make mistakes and have set backs. There's not a person on this planet that has a different story in the world of entrepreneurialism. And who knows, maybe one day you'll write a book, telling others about your experience. Continue learning and laughing, especially at yourself, because there will be some comical moments, I promise you. Starting a business isn't for the weak, but remember your why and remain consistent. The rewards are plentiful.

We've come to the end of this book, but hopefully the beginning of your dreams are being realized! I hope I've inspired you to move forward. If so, I'm excited you have the audacity to do what many are reluctant to do – to start the damn business! Don't forget to check out the resources I've added in the next section to help you get started. Hopefully you'll answer the call for greatness and walk out a level of success that was meant for you in this realm. Some won't – but I'm depending on you to do so. The world is waiting.

I love you.

NICCI CANADA
Author. Speaker. Entrepreneur

BUSINESS RESOURCES

It's time to focus and get to work! To help you get started, I have collected valuable resources and compiled them on my website. (Click the "Business Resources" tab)

You'll find:

- Start Up Check List
- Start Up Resources
- Business Resources (by state)
- And More!

PLEASE DO YOUR RESEARCH, read over materials thoroughly and choose things that are best suitable for your business needs. I believe in you.

www.shutupandstartthedamnbusiness.com

Greatness looks good on you.

- Nicci Canada